THE
FALL
of the
GIANT

WRITTEN & ILLUSTRATED

BY

NOURA DURKEE

THE FALL
of the
GIANT

Published by:
Tahrike Tarsile Quran Inc.
Publishers and Distributors of The Qur'an
P.O. Box 731115
Elmhurst, New York 11373-0115

author & illustrator: Noura Durkee

First U.S. Edition 1999
Library of Congress Catalog Number: 98-061664
British Library Cataloguing in Publication Data
ISBN: 1-879402-63-7

The Prophet Daud ﷺ is mentioned in the Qur'an
in chapters 2:249-251, 6:84, 21:78-80, 34:10-11, 38:17-26.

Muslims always ask the blessings of Allah
on the prophets and some others,
whenever the name of the person is mentioned.
Blessings used in this story are:
ﷺ : 'alayhi-s-salam: peace be upon him

Daud ﷺ was a shepherd.
His job was to take care of the sheep.
He kept them together
and found the lost ones.

He helped them if they got hurt.

He chased away wolves and lions that wanted to eat them up.

But most of the time, he walked with them over the rocky hills, looking for good grass. When they found it, he sat and watched them eat. Sheep love to eat, a little here, a little there. So he spent a lot of time sitting and watching.

He thought about everything.
He looked at the mountains and rocks and
flowers. He saw the many million animals
and bugs and plants Allah has made.
He was very amazed.

He opened his mouth,
and Allah taught him songs to sing.
He carved flutes and blew them.
The music lifted up from the valleys,
and traveled into the sky.
Daud ﷺ sang about everything:
the hills, the rocks,the trees, the sheep.
Daud ﷺ sang about
not being afraid of anything.
He sang about loving and serving Allah.

The songs were so beautiful
that the mountians
echoed them
back to the sky.

His songs were so beautiful and full of hope
that the birds wanted to sing with him.
They gathered together in big flocks
and joined their songs with his.

So at sunrise and in the evening,
Daud ﷺ and the birds
and the mountains
sang and praised Allah.

Daud ﷺ went on peacefully singing
and taking care of his sheep.
He had two things to help him in his
work.
One was a staff, a long strong stick
(with a bend at the end).
What can you do with a long strong stick

(with a bend at the end)
?

You can lean on it.

You can walk with it.

You can move bushes aside
to make a path.   high

You can reach things up

You can even spank a sheep,
if it is naughty.

And you can rescue that sheep
if it gets stuck
in a hard place.

Daud ﷺ also had a sling.
His sling was just a long piece of
leather that wrapped around a
smooth stone.

He would hold the two ends
and swing it around his head,
faster and faster, like this:
swoop, swoop, swish, swap!
As he let go one end, the stone would
go flying wherever he wanted it to.
He used to practice hitting rocks.
He got very good at it.

If any animal bothered his sheep, SNAP! A stone would hit it HARD. So the sheep were safe with Daud ﷺ.

At that time the king of the country
was fighting a war against a big army.
It was a strong army with lots of soldiers.
Their leader was a very VERY big man.

He was bigger than anybody.
He was so big people called him a GIANT.
His head stuck up above all the heads
of all the other soldiers.

He was very strong, too.
Everybody was scared of him.
His name was Jaloot.

When Daud ﷺ heard about the war he thought,
"Well, I have my staff and my sling.
Maybe I can help."
So he left his sheep and he went with the army
to fight. He was a teen-ager at the time.

The soldiers went along and went along
until they were near the other army.
They came to a stream.

King Taloot said, "Whoever is with us, don't drink! Or just drink a handful." This was a test for them.

A few of the soldiers obeyed the king.
They didn't drink anything.
Daud ﷺ was with them.
But most of the army drank a lot.

But most of the army drank a lot.
They were very thirsty.
They didn't pay attention to their king.

Then when they crossed the river,
the drinkers got very weak and scared.
They said,
"We can't fight Jaloot and his army today!
He is too big and they are too many!"

The faithful soldiers said,
"A small group can beat a large one!
Allah stays with the ones who don't give up!"

So they asked Allah to make them brave,
and they went on.
But who could fight Jaloot?
He was VERY big and
VERY STRONG!!

Jaloot stood in front of his army and dared *anyone* to fight him.

The king said, "Who will fight Jaloot? Who?"
Nobody volunteered.
Nobody wanted to do it.

Daud ﷺ said, "With Allah's help, I'll do it!"
Everybody laughed at him.
"You're only a shepherd boy!" they said. "You aren't even a soldier! You don't have a sword!"
But the king had no one else.
So he offered Daud ﷺ his own sword to fight with.

"No, thank you," said Daud ﷺ.
"I know how to use my staff and
my sling. I'll just take them."

He chose five smooth stones
and walked out to fight Jaloot.

Jaloot stood on the field, shouting with his
great loud voice and waving his great big
sharp sword. He looked down at Daud ﷺ.

Who was this little person?
Everybody was afraid of Jaloot.
What was this boy doing with his stick and his
sling? Did he think he could fight with them?

Daud ﷺ looked up at Jaloot. He measured the
distance between them carefully, and picked
out one flat stone. He put it in the sling, and
twirled it round and round, faster and faster,
faster*fasterfasterfaster* until...

It hit him SMACK between the eyes,
and knocked him out.
Jaloot fell with a
gigantic,
stupendous

CRASH!!

His falling felt like an earthquake!

Daud 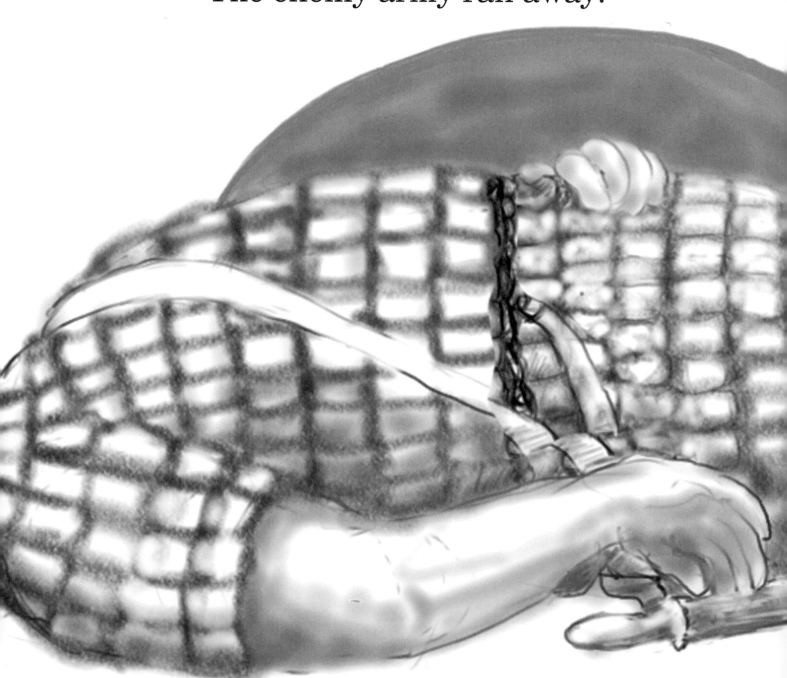 stepped up, grasped Jaloot's own sword,
and cut off his head.
That was that.
The enemy army ran away.

King Taloot took Daud ﷺ back with him to his palace. He taught him how to be the next king. A very good king he became, too. He had to give up watching his sheep, and take care of the people instead.

But whenever he could, Daud ﷺ would go out into the hills, and sing to Allah.

The birds and the hills sang with him.

the end